RELATE:
A Guide to Marriage & Relationship Repair

Recharge your romance
Energize your love life
Laugh together
Accept your differences
Transform through trials
Engage one another

Christa Hardin, MA

A Reflections Counseling Center Publication

RELATE: A Guide to Marriage & Relationship Repair

RELATE: A Guide to Marriage & Relationship Repair
Copyright © 2013 by Christa M. Hardin
All rights reserved. This book or any portion thereof
may not be reproduced or used in any manner whatsoever
without the express written permission of the publisher
except for the use of brief quotations in a book review.
Printed in the United States of America
First Printing, 2013
ISBN 1491015209

Reflections Counseling Center
630 S. Orange
Sarasota, Fl 34236
www.reflectionscc.com

We hope you enjoy this Reflections Counseling Center publication. Our goal is to create and promote writings that will bring health, hope, and healing to those who read them. If you have any questions or comments about this book, write to us at reflectionscounselingcenter@gmail.com

Contents

Foreword..5

Chapter 1: Recharge Your Romance........................7

Chapter 2: Energize Your Love Life.........................17

Chapter 3: Laugh Together......................................29

Chapter 4: Accept Your Differences........................37

Chapter 5: Transform Through Trials......................43

Chapter 6: Engage One Another..............................53

Chapter 7: Ready, Set, Repair!..................................61

FOREWORD

Are you ready to RELATE?

RELATE is a simple, refreshing, and effective relationship repair program. Designed by a marital expert, RELATE helps couples to work together to create the relationship they've always wanted. When a couple is relating well together, they can thrive in the world far better than the two of them could have done on their own. The steps to relate better in this book can be worked on individually, as a couple, or together with a coach or counselor.

RELATE is designed to aid a couple that is stressed, overloaded, bored, or otherwise desperate for more relationship satisfaction. This program focuses specifically on restoring lost feelings of love or respect for one another, on reminding a couple of their greater commitment to God and their spouses and families, and on building them up to be a solid team once again, or even for the first time.

RELATE can help even if just one member of a relationship wants to participate while the other is doubtful or uninterested in change. A willing mate can make a great change in a relationship by trying new steps respectfully. It is often the case that both members of the relationship are committed to the relationship, but only one wants help. As most counselors know, when even one person makes healthy changes, a relational system often shifts in a positive direction.

RELATE is NOT for the couple that is uncommitted or unwilling to take part in change. Examples of this are where one or both mates are in complete withdrawal from the relationship, when one partner is happily caught up in an affair, when an individual is in an abusive relationship, or in other extreme situations. In these instances, individuals and couples should pursue therapy or outside help more intensively and specifically tailored to their issues.

Here are five essentials to getting the most out of this book:

- Read the material *carefully*. This program is designed to be efficient already, so simply skimming this book will leave a gap in your relationship repair.
- Do the assignments. They're not complicated, but they do take effort, like anything worth doing. Passively reading a book about your issues is not going to be the magical solution. The key to success lies not only in your momentary participation, but also in your *lasting efforts* in working toward a healthier relationship.
- Don't give up before the end! This is a short training program, so finish it fully. Do your best, and expect great results. Even if your mate isn't dedicated, keep it up. You can't lose when you are trying to love others and yourself well!
- Pay special attention to the heading **"LOVE NOTES"** that you find sprinkled throughout the book. These brief tips will help you to make sure you consider your mates' feelings and express love toward them even when you don't agree on everything.
- Expect success and have fun! Keep an attitude of hopefulness and celebrate even the smallest of positive changes! Soon, you will be celebrating a lifetime of love.

Now let's get started!

CHAPTER 1

RECHARGE YOUR ROMANCE

Remember how much fun and passion you experienced with your mate when your relationship first began? Do you ever wonder what happened to it? If so, you are not alone. Most couples go through a similar experience, even if not everyone admits to it. Though decreased romantic feelings are often typical over the years, you don't have to follow the path to marital ruin like many others unwittingly do. You can fuel the fires of intimacy and fun so you don't end up burning out before the finish line, where the wonderful relationship you have always dreamed about is waiting!

To get started on a relationship recharge, spend some time reflecting on what it is you enjoyed about your mate when you first came together. List at least five different things. Examples are their kindness, good looks, sense of humor, fitness level, intelligence, faith, money management skills, etc., even if they no longer apply!

What did I enjoy most about my mate in the beginning?

1. _____
2. _____
3. _____
4. _____
5. _____

Share this list with your mate during a quiet moment. Don't ask them to share their list with you yet. Just enjoy your own memories for a few minutes. You may find that positive emotions are beginning to resurface from this rekindling.

Of course, doing this exercise alone cannot begin to address where you find yourselves now. In fact, you may now wonder more than ever why you chose your mate. Either way, would you like to feel better about your significant other? If so, be honest with yourself and your significant other in this book and keep going. There is *always* hope for your relationship so long as *you* haven't given up.

Now take an honest relationship survey and spend a few moments writing down or thinking about the ways you struggle as a couple currently. Of course you won't have room for every tiny detail, but list up to five of the largest things hindering your relationship now.

LOVE NOTE: *You and your mate may not agree even on the things hindering your relationship. That's ok for now, just keep moving ahead. Allow your mate the space to process the relationship the way he or she sees it, just as you have the freedom to do.*

What is hindering our relationship?

1. _____
2. _____
3. _____
4. _____
5. _____

This is another great list to talk over with a coach or therapist during your next session. It lists your relationship difficulties very concretely, and when the issues themselves can often seem so out of control, it is healthy to see them in list format and shortened down to a few statements, however big or small they may feel.

Now that you can clearly see most of the issues in your relationship, spend a few moments thinking about the goals for its repair. Surely you don't expect the exact replica of what you once had when your love was new and there were not as many bills, responsibilities, or the same family concerns, considering you are doubtlessly older and have different life experiences than you once did. However, there is now hope for new, wonderful things that fit better with the people you both are today.

List some realistic goals for your marriage or relationship, but also allow some dreaming room! What would you like to see happen in your relationship? What will it take to revitalize your relationship?

LOVE NOTE: *As your mate shares, try to offer an attitude of openness and gratefulness for their vulnerability in sharing versus an attitude of resentment if you hear about dreams and goals that differ from your own. After all, your mate will likely cut you off from hearing about their dreams and goals for the relationship if you are cold and harsh toward them in this moment of vulnerability. Worse, they may stop dreaming about the goals altogether.*

What do we want for our relationship?

1. _____
2. _____
3. _____
4. _____
5. _____

If you completed this list on your own, share your hopes and dreams for the relationship with your spouse or partner and find out if he or she has any new dreams or feels congruent with yours. Usually there is some overlap but some of the goals of each individual may surprise and offer hope to the other.

Use the space on the next page to consolidate any *mutual goals* you both wrote or agreed upon. Don't be discouraged if none of your goals were the same. When you get past this common problem, it's important to recognize that although some of the ways you go about trying to reach your mutual goals differ, you *are* on the same team! If you can't find any mutual goals after talking it through for a moment, get down to very basic goals that you both share for the relationship, such as "To create a peaceful, hard-working, and yet fun environment for our family," or "To create a relationship where we fight less frequently, and enjoy one another more."

What are our goals for our relationship?

1. _____
2. _____
3. _____
4. _____
5. _____

CONSTRUCTING OUR RELATIONSHIP TIMELINE

Now, it's time to become a historian of your relationship with your spouse or mate. Plug in some figures for the timeline below to recollect different "eras" of your relationship. Relationships evolve and grow as life changes, and they grow either lush and full, like a prized rose collection, or more sparse and frail, like a flower in an untended or abandoned garden. Like most flowers, relationships change and bloom more fully in some seasons than others, as well as often have elements of both death and life, so make sure you don't judge yourself too harshly if there are less flowering seasons than you would like. Those days are coming again soon! This is just a roadmap of the relationship so your therapist, pastor, accountability couple, and especially *you*, can see it a bit more clearly.

The spaces on the next page are numbered and can represent years, months, or time periods, for example "When the kids were in diapers." It does not matter how you categorize the list as long as *you* know what the timeline represents. Try to find some positive events and some negative events to note, and also things that have contributed to you being steadier as a couple. Examples of positive events could be something you are proud of, like "Our wedding day," or "Five year anniversary weekend away," or when you successfully moved out of state or graduated from a program that helped your family. Negative events may be when one mate started working a difficult shift, when there was a financial or health crisis (or both), or when a marriage or child's issues became overwhelming. Try to consolidate the list to about seven or eight things that were difficult, and seven or eight that were positive if possible. If not, feel free to use another space to record the list. Accuracy is after all, more important than keeping to a specific design.

Our Relationship Timeline

1. _____
2. _____
3. _____
4. _____
5. _____
6. _____
7. _____
8. _____
9. _____
10. _____
11. _____
12. _____
13. _____
14. _____
15. _____

TIMELINE REVIEW

After seeing your relationship's main events written down, it's probably evident that while you've had some good times, it's not always been an easy road. As you look at this list together or on your own, go ahead and take a few deep breaths, commit your relationship to God, and thank Him for the good things you listed. Now take a few more deep breaths, and ask Him to give you strength to work on the other areas, the problem areas. *You* are going to continue to do your best and pray for strength, but ask and trust God to do His part too. Remember that by being stressed and worried, you cannot help anything. Stress and worry over your relationship will only cause you to grow wearier, more frustrated and even depressed. This stress may even increase your risks for ulcers, headaches, and even certain cancers or heart disease.

The next part of recharging your romance includes assessing to find out the problems causing the drain in your relationship. We've done this a little bit already by inspecting your relationship from an organized, practical perspective and discovering in which ways it has drained you both. Next, recharging involves working to bring life back into your relationship!

Now take a moment to flip back to the list you wrote regarding the things that caused an attraction to your spouse or mate. Take a few minutes to think about what it was about *you* that really cinched it for your significant other. You can ask them to list five things if you prefer, but you probably know them anyway. Think about them or ask your partner, and then write them here.

Why did my spouse fall for me?

1. _____
2. _____
3. _____
4. _____
5. _____

As you look over the list, do you think you still resemble the person you once were when he or she fell for you? Maybe you aren't the same, and wouldn't want to be, but most of the things on the list are probably good qualities that you enjoy remembering about yourself. Maybe you feel very positive after making the list because you still feel like you possess these character traits, or maybe you are a little discouraged wondering how you could ever be like that again since you've since been through so much since then. Whatever the case, in order to truly recharge this relationship, you *do* need to acknowledge the great things about you that may have gotten lost along the way!

A wonderful step toward bringing out the best in yourself and to beginning the recharge process is to **try each day to do one thing to be like the person you were when your spouse fell in love with you**. Externally, you are older and you certainly shouldn't try to reverse the hands of time, but youthfulness is beautifully seen in an older person as well as young, so don't let age stop you from feeling like you can be attractive! Besides youthfulness, other examples couples who have tried this exercise have given are that their mate fell in love with them because they were kind, thoughtful, organized, took good care of themselves physically, had a positive attitude, wore great clothes and makeup, were affectionate, had a great sense of humor, were a hard worker, or were adventurous, to name a few. Though all of the reasons your significant other fell for you may not seem possible now, at least most of the things spouses record about one another are still doable, which should be very encouraging for you!

To reiterate, this recharge task invites you to try to make an effort to be like the person your spouse fell in love with, at least once a day, in a way that feels comfortable and congruent with who you are today. You have *nothing* to lose by trying to be a better and more naturally attractive person inside and out, so go for it! One thing a day is an easy goal to meet!

LOVE NOTE: *Don't ask you spouse to keep score or to notice whether you are succeeding in trying to behave differently, or it could get ugly. Let the change be obvious enough to speak for itself!*

MY LANGUAGE FOR LOVE

Before we move on, one final list in this chapter is just as important as the others. It targets ways that *you* feel most loved most by your spouse. *You* may not even know your favorite ways to feel loved by your spouse, and if *you* don't know, how can they know? Consider the question of when you feel most loved for a moment. Is it when he or she scratches your back, reads aloud to you, cleans the house, is considerate of your sexual desires, listens to you, plays your favorite sport or video game with you, works out with you, enjoys the same music or art as you, takes you on fun dates, plays with the kids, works hard for you, or something else? List the top five specific ways you enjoy feeling loved by your spouse here.

What are my favorite ways of being loved?

1. _____
2. _____
3. _____

4. _____
5. _____

Now try to get your significant other to share his or her favorite ways to feel loved by you. If he or she is unwilling, write down the ways you think you can love your mate the best here.

What are my mate's favorite ways to be loved?

1. _____
2. _____
3. _____
4. _____
5. _____

Now, for both practical and romantic reasons, try loving your significant other in their favorite ways! If he or she is doing this book with you, ask them to try to do the same for you. If you feel overwhelmed by their list, try to love them in just one of these ways each day. Now review the main points of this chapter, and begin the wonderful recharging of your relationship!

REVIEW: RECHARGE PLAN FOR YOUR RELATIONSHIP

1. Complete the lists in this chapter, and if your significant other is willing to participate, ask him or her to do their lists and then share them together.
2. Spend time doing (or trying to do) one thing each day that encouraged your spouse to fall in love with you. If you forget a day, just try the next. Do not brag about what you are doing, just do it.
3. Do not become obsessed about the list of problems you or your mate listed. You've spent plenty of time thinking about these things and recharging is an important first step, since your emotional batteries may be drained. Worrying will not help, nor will trying to work from an exhausted and overwhelmed perspective! Let's bring life back into the relationship for now, so tackling the harder issues in a later chapter will be easier.

4. Spend time this week trying to love your mate in his or her favorite ways. Pray for God to give you wisdom about this! In James we read that He promises to give wisdom to anyone who seeks it (James 1:5).

While you move onto learning more from other chapters, keep doing the Recharge Plan items until they become a habit. Habits often takes twenty-one days to form, but as noted earlier, being an attractive person inside and out is something to hang on to, as is loving others well, so don't stop making efforts after twenty-one days. Get used to this healthier way of living and loving. What happens if you don't feel energized or motivated to do this? Well, let's move on to keeping the energy up in your relationship!

CHAPTER 2

ENERGIZE YOUR LOVE LIFE

In our last chapter, you learned how to give your relationship a jumpstart. It's fairly easy to recharge your emotional batteries, but it's hard work to *keep* the energy current running steadily through it. In fact, one definition of hard work is *a change in energy forces*. In other words, you need to put plenty of energy *into* your relationship to get anything worthwhile from it. Now it's time to keep the momentum going, and there are many great ways of doing just that.

PRIORITIZE RELATE RELATIONSHIP TIME

One great way to keep energy in your relationship is to assess how much time you are putting into one other. Is your relationship a priority in your schedule right now? Well, ask yourself. Is there any *specific* time set aside for the relationship? It may sounds silly to set aside time for it if you are a couple who does not lead a busy life or have children running around, but even for those couples who are not busy, you still need time to set aside for this important relationship, *especially* if it's stressed. Whether you are busy or just simply stressed in your relating, how much time do you think, on average, you put into building up your relationship with your spouse, arguing aside? Write it down here.

I put _____ hours into energizing our relationship per week.

Whatever the number of hours you actively put into your relationship currently, **couples should ideally spend ten hours a week energizing their relationship.** Out of approximately one hundred and fifteen waking hours, ten hours are only a small fraction of them, and should be protected, maintained, and spent together having RELATE time.

It's time for the two of you to discuss some times and ways to connect and build energy into the relationship. These times should have four basic rules.

1. Couples should be physically touching or looking at each other (or both, even better!) during at least some of this time.
2. Couples should be alone at least a fair amount of the time. If you are home and have small children getting out of bed, interruptions may be expected.
3. Couples should not discuss problems during this time. Problems can be talked about at other times of course, but during this special RELATE time, problems should not intentionally be discussed, although if something comes up on an occasional time, don't keep score. Just make sure it stays basically free of problems, so you can honor that time.
4. Couples should ideally find something to do together that both enjoy to some degree.

Now that we've established some basic rules about your RELATE time, build a list of fun things you like doing together. Make sure to include physical time together, emotional time together, and if both are willing, spiritual time together:

What are some fun things we can do together?

1. _____
2. _____
3. _____
4. _____
5. _____
6. _____
7. _____
8. _____
9. _____
10. _____

LOVE NOTE: *Here is a sample list of things that can be done inexpensively at home or on a local date, depending on the season and your personal calendars and interests. For a more extensive list, see the "Resources" page at www.ReflectionsCC.com.*

- Playing a favorite board game with a snack you enjoy.
- Physical intimacy (As you grow closer, both spouses can share their ideas for making this area better also, such as creating a romantic setting, sharing favorite techniques, etc.).
- Watching a show together while you cuddle or trade turns back scratching.
- Listening to new and old favorite songs together.
- Going to a favorite restaurant.
- Having a bake-off with sweet treats.
- Playing a sport against each other.
- Going for walks or jogs or getting into shape together.
- Having a picnic.
- Working on a fun project together.
- Going on a "date" that interests you both.
- Doing a puzzle together.
- Taking a dance class together.

Though many times, a couple does not get a chance to have a quote on quote "date night" every week, you can easily try for some of the above strategies several times a week, even if you're still building up to the goal of ten hours a week. If you are not working opposite shifts or travelling frequently, the good news is, with a little planning, the ten hours of RELATE time together should be completely doable. The truth is, if you aren't willing to set aside something else a few times a week to focus on your relationship, you really can't expect any lasting results.

After reading the above ideas and adding your own ideas to the mix, make a short list of things you will try doing together, and share *when* you will try doing them. Many couples do a sitter swap with other couples with children from church or work so they can get free babysitting for the out and about dates or hire a local teen from church or the YMCA to sit. A date could be as simple as sharing a foot-long sub, a bags of chips, a piece of fruit, and a pack of cards, just so long as you set aside the time together and you generally avoid talking about problems. After making the list, brainstorm some more, and then refine the list with your mate if possible, so you have a list that works for both of you. Once you get through the initial lists and start spending time together in this problem-free zone, the RELATE time will probably be one the most satisfying times in your week, and your list will grow to add all sorts of fun times together. You may even find a new hobby, or remember an old pastime in the efforts you make. Enjoy!

WHEN WE WILL MAKE IT HAPPEN

Now that you know the importance of RELATE time together and you have some mutual ideas to try out, it's time to really focus on *when* it will happen. Examples are listed below, but use your own schedule to build your unique relationship time.

- After the kids are in bed on time (and one or both of us will put them to bed on time).
- We will go to the gym together and put the kids in childcare.
- We will bring the kids to church or a sitter's house mid-week or on a weekend and go to dinner.
- I will send her an email or text several mornings a week to remind her of our late night plans.
- We will connect during a child's sport or lesson.
- I will tell him I'm getting the kids to bed with a movie or book early Fridays and Sundays so we can have our time together.
- I will call a few friends to arrange for sitter swaps.
- When we first get home from work (or after dinner) we will avoid talking about the more stressful aspects of our days, and focus on thankfulness for being together.

Use the next space to arrange for when you and your spouse will generally set aside time for RELATE time. Don't get discouraged if it changes, or doesn't follow a pattern. As long as it happens, you are on the right track!

When will we make it happen?

1. _____
2. _____
3. _____

LOVE NOTE: *If you are married and your spouse does not want to spend time planning to love you well, don't withhold your love and commitment to them. Surprise them even more by loving them well anyway. Pray that they will be influenced by your loving ways. Do your best to recognize the many ways they do love you even if they're not as obvious, such as going to work for the family, helping with household responsibilities, or loving or caring for the children. This love and then wait-and-see attitude isn't always easy to carry out, but it is worth doing! In fact, the "give and take in exactly equal portions" plan is actually less loving since it is a "tit for tat" mentality. If you want true love in your relationship, you can have it. True love does not count and measure. Read 1st Corinthians 13:4-7 to hear this specifically. Love because you are loved by God, and so is your partner. You can still personally thrive by loving a spouse or partner well by remembering this and by also making sure to get self-care in other ways (see SELF CARE TIPS heading later in this chapter).*

KEEPING HEALTHY ATTITUDES DURING CONFLICTS

Now that you have some ideas for making time in your relationship and have established some no-stress RELATE time, let's talk about keeping energy flowing in your relationship by increasing your healthy attitudes during conflict.

Let's face it, if you can't stop arguing all day, and you try avoiding problems at night for RELATE time, you may not be able to enjoy one another authentically sometimes. If you have lots of conflict, don't give up! Most couples have found relief and have kept a healthier attitude by knowing that they have the sacred ten hours a week set aside even if they are at battle during other parts of the week. In any case, read on for dealing with conflict in a healthy manner, so that all of your days and nights can be a whole lot less stressful!

HOW YOU TYPICALLY DEAL WITH CONFLICT

Here are three common conflict styles. Do you find yourself in this list, or do you have another way of handling stress in your relationship? Write in one of your own typical conflict patterns if you can't find yours here:

1. Avoidance of the problem by one or both mates.
2. Yelling and screaming.
3. Being passive aggressive (with manipulation or withholding).
4. _____

Many couples do not fit any specific conflict pattern and have days or seasons where they are more sullen and withdrawn in their relationship, whereas at other times they yell, badger, or manipulate. Some find themselves using all of the above unhealthy conflict styles in the very same argument. In fact, sometimes conflict is so emotionally laden that it is difficult for one or both mates to even properly label or remember what typically happens. If you are discouraged by your current conflict patterns, you don't have to stay there!

CHOOSE DIGNITY & RESPECT

As a person who has doubtlessly loved you during many difficult seasons of life (or at the very least, is still and always a child of God), your significant other deserves the dignity and respect you are capable of offering, even if you feel frustrated or scared and want to withhold or lash out. As a matter of fact, you also owe it to yourself to incorporate healthier ways of behaving. Holding in your feelings, avoiding things until you burst, or screaming at the top of your lungs are terrible ways of keeping *you* healthy physically and emotionally, regardless of whether you feel like your spouse or mate deserves to be punished. Instead of finger pointing at yourself or your mate, use your time in this book to receive better ways of dealing with conflict. The healthy, non-draining ways of solving problems take some real effort, but the beautiful result is worth every bit of energy you put into it.

Note the following practices of healthy emotional discussion when couples are hurt or frustrated:

- If you find yourself yelling or using combative language, scale back and use the words, "I feel…" instead of "You are…" or "You make me feel…" "I" language keeps the focus on your own struggles and doesn't accuse.
- When an issue becomes emotionally laden, keep your tone down to a whisper so you can keep your heart rate and blood pressure down and in turn, influence your mate to avoid escalating to a yell. It's hard to yell at someone who is whispering!
- Make the choice never to bring the words "divorce" into your conversation, since threatening to end your love totally encourages the committed spouse to feel threatened and to withdraw.
- Remove all forms of name-calling from your marriage. Bullying has never won anyone real love, but only brings pity or fear.
- If your mate continues to calls you a name after you've set the "no name calling" boundary, take a breather and talk to a trusted counselor.
- Take some deep breaths, pray quietly, and/or do some stretches in the midst of the argument to keep your body from reading your mental stress and making things worse. By doing this, you avoid potential ulcers, headaches, crying fits, and others ways we physically break down when our system gets overwhelmed. Deep breathing, prayer, and stretching keep your body in a non-emergency stance, and allow your significant other to know that while the argument is important, you still maintain a level of self-care and respect towards yourself and their personhood as well, despite your frustrations. Asking God for help in a difficult moment is a pretty great idea all-around, too!
- Be a good listener! Slow down and mirror back what you have heard your spouse saying if you start to freak out, so you can make sure you are hearing him or her correctly. Sometimes when you are frustrated or emotional, you could miss what was really said.

- Write texts, letters or emails to your mate, telling him or her how you are feeling about a frustration, making sure never to give (or press 'send') unless you think you could be happy with the letter in the future, and know that it wouldn't be seen as incriminating in any way. Those emotionally laden letters can certainly be written also for the purpose of releasing anger, as long as they are deleted or torn up afterwards, since you typically don't want to record an angry outburst in most cases. Remember as you write that written words can be perceived with a different tone than you intend. Therefore, try to use plenty of loving words in addition to expressing your frustrations in a logical manner. Finish each letter with a sentiment of love, which often leaves your mate more likely to consider your opinion, versus retaliating out of fear of abandonment.
- If you don't think you can do any of the above steps in the midst of an argument, let your significant other know you are going to take a breather. Make sure you tell them you care about them, but that you need to take care of yourself so you don't get too stressed. It's much better to own your own emotions than say, "Because you are too awful…"
- Try to end each fight by saying, "I love you and am committed to you," even if you haven't reached a satisfying resolution.
- Don't let your preconceived notions of what should happen after an argument dictate your life. Remember, each and every moment is precious, so if the two of you feel like being intimate, laughing, going to dinner, or renting a movie, enjoy the special time even if the argument did not get completely resolved. If we are honest with ourselves, most of our arguments as adults don't have a complete resolution, simply because some things are a matter of preference or choice and are not "black and white" or "clear-cut" issues with easy solutions.
- Add ideas of your own here that you'd like to try or that have worked in the past for when you are having a conflict in your relationship (ex: praying together, seeing a counselor, walking while we talk in public, sleeping on it, giving ourselves a time limit and then planning something fun afterwards, compromising, etc):

_____
_____
_____
_____

USING THE CONFLICT MANAGEMENT TACTICS

Now that you are learning more about healthy ways to relate, are focusing more on your spouse's best qualities, are remembering that you are on the same team and not divided, and are incorporating RELATE time into your life together, you should be ready to review your earlier list regarding the biggest problems hindering you in your marriage or relationship. Revisit the list of things hindering your relationship that you wrote down in Chapter One on page 8 and if those are still your biggest problems, use the tools for healthy conflict in the previous pages to try to talk through them. Don't bring something up if it isn't good timing, or if things are improving from your other efforts. If this is the case, talk about those problems when and if they come up again, and revisit the tools you learned here on an as-needed basis.

SETTING A BOUNDARY DURING THE CONFLICT

If your mate feels the problems need to be discussed right away, but you don't want to pursue the argument until later, honor their desires to talk about it if you are in a private setting. However, if you really aren't ready, give them a specific time when you will talk about it, and follow through. For example, say, "I'll be ready to talk when the kids are asleep (or in their rooms for the night.)" If, when you are arguing, there is no progress being made, let your mate know that you want to move on after a certain time has passed, resolution or not. Examples of boundary setting in this way are, "Ok, if you want to talk about it, that's fine. I need to start winding down and relaxing in ten minutes, though." Stick to your plans and offer a hug, kind words, or a smile before leaving the room or the topic, so your spouse knows that you love them. Make sure you allow your spouse time to cool off if he or she needs to, if you are planning some relationship time afterwards. If you are planning for RELATE time afterwards, do your best to choose something that will lift the mood and not require as much effort until one or both of you can cool down. Examples not requiring much effort are watching a movie together, having a dinner out together, reading a book aloud together, or just scratching one another's backs quietly before bed. If you have to leave for work, send an email or text saying you love your partner after you arrive. Don't get into a "texting war," if they respond unkindly. Keep your boundary by waiting until after your day allows for some time to process things and trust God for the result. Don't panic that your spouse or partner will be upset with you. You have to take care of your family and responsibilities and it is okay to compartmentalize if you are using healthy methods and not avoiding the problem altogether.

STILL DISCOURAGED ABOUT CONFLICT?

If none of the earlier conflict management styles help you to feel less emotionally upset, or you can't seem to get a grip, it may be because you are so needy and dependent on your mate for your needs to be met, that you are panicking whenever there is conflict. Instead of thinking rationally, you are groping and controlling, since you so strongly fear rejection from this person you have allowed to become your every reason for living. If this is you, do not condemn yourself but realize you simply need more self-care.

LOVE NOTE: *Even if you have a loving and healthy spouse, if you are one hundred percent dependent on your mate for your needs to be met, you are going to feel disappointment on a regular basis. Only God can fill the ultimate restlessness we feel since we were created for relationship with Him.*

SELF CARE TIPS

Even if you have a great conflict style, if you want to bring more energy into your life together, you need to make sure you are taking good care of yourself. As in the example of putting on your own oxygen mask first in an airplane disaster, you need to *have* something to give emotionally, before you can expect loving others to come more naturally. Try praying, reading your Bible and other edifying books, listening to uplifting music, exercising, and spending time with others who care about you, get started on a hobby, seek counseling, or get medical attention to make sure you are healthy. In other words, give yourself the gift of learning to love God, yourself and others well before you expect to have energy for your relationships building.

If you aren't naturally getting self-care, write a simple list with three columns like this each day:

Spiritual Self Care   **Emotional Self Care**   **Physical Self Care**

Do at least one thing in each of these columns per day, so you will have energy for your own wellness, and so you will have something to give to your mate and others. For example, one day may look like the one below for a person with a full-time job and children. Your own list may look completely different from this or look different each day, since mixing it up is even more fun!

1. Spiritual Self Care: Monday: Listened to audio Bible and prayed on the way to work, Tuesday: Read Bible and listened to worship song.
2. Emotional Self Care: Monday: Took a long, hot bath with a magazine after the kids were in bed, Tuesday: Went out for coffee with a friend.
3. Physical Self Care: Monday: Did fifty stomach exercises before bed, Tuesday: Went for a brisk walk with the dog before work.

REVIEW: ENERGIZE PLAN FOR YOUR RELATIONSHIP

1. Take ten or more hours a week to love your mate actively, using the completed lists in this chapter for your RELATE time together. Make sure you plan for this time to happen or it may slip away.
2. Practice new and better ways of dealing with conflict and commit to stopping the usage of the unhealthy patterns. Get counseling or accountability help as needed. Take breaks as needed. Look back at your list of the things hindering your relationship when the timing is right, and practice your new conflict management skills.

3. Get better self-care, so you have authentic energy to put into the relationship, and don't expect your mate to meet all of your needs. Most importantly, allow your life with God to grow richer as you trust Him to heal your marriage.

Because you will likely be spending more time together as a result of your decision to actively recharge and follow the Energize Plan in your marriage, let's talk about some ways to have fun together throughout the week, so you can thoroughly look forward to and enjoy the time you've now set apart. Read about this in the next chapter, "Laugh Together."

CHAPTER 3

Laugh together

When you choose to relate better with your significant other, one of the best ways you can build the relationship is to laugh together. Many couples that don't have much fun often wonder why other couples seem to laugh so naturally together. Many times, couples that are laughing together aren't just laughing because it always comes naturally. In fact, it is often intentional, as in the, "We'd rather laugh than cry," philosophy some people choose to live out. Maybe they laugh together because they've made the conscious choice to be optimists instead of pessimists. Maybe they realize life is short, or it is because of an overflow of joy and mirth and a deep trust in the Lord's provision despite their temporary annoyances with their spouse. In many other cases, laughter seems natural for a couple because they came from living in an environment where laughter was modeled for them, and they were blessed to gain this type of laughing legacy. Unfortunately, laughter can also stem from an indulgent, inebriated, or mean-spirited nature, in which case the relationship will inevitably come to its own demise in some way, shape or form, even if it's not plain to others.

In any case whether it comes naturally to you or not, it's definitely worth seeking out an honest, clean type of fun together. This is because laughter is vital to the health of a relationship. One of the best-kept secrets of a good team is that although the team plays their best collectively, the team members know not to take themselves or the game too seriously, but to keep an element of fun in it.

Even if your spouse or mate doesn't want to seek out laughter in your relationship, it is still an important goal for you. You still want joy and physical health, right? You also want a happier relationship, right?

If so, bringing humor into the relationship yourself may rub off on the other person, but even if you are the only one blessed with a newfound sparkle of fun in the relationship, you are blessed indeed. Long after the flower of romance fades, as it does for many a healthy and committed couple, a sense of humor can connect them for life.

Even if you are already pretty good at humor, you are reading this book because you want more health in the relationship, so let's dig up something funny up again! I want you to take a moment to remember three things that have been funny in your relationship, even if they were long ago. Try to find things that were funny to both of you, but were not at the expense of your mate, such as, "When that mud slung onto your face during the snowball fight, it was priceless!" You might have funny parenting moments that make you smile or laugh now, even if at the time they were painful, you may have planned a surprise for your spouse that was fun, visited a comedy club, acted together in a mystery dinner game, watched a hilarious movie, or read a funny book together. Take a moment to list a few funny memories, even if they are not your "Top Funniest Moments" as a couple.

What are some of our funniest moments together?

1. _____
2. _____
3. _____
4. _____
5. _____

Now, take a moment to share your list with your mate. Take some time to talk about examples he or she remembers being funny, and try not to be sensitive if he or she mentions something that wasn't as funny to you. There is already plenty of conflict in life, so don't bring it in now. As for fun and humor in your relationship, here are plenty of ideas for bringing more humor out in a healthy way. Choose some off the list or add your own underneath, and spend some of your ten RELATE hours each week trying to bring these types of fun into it!

FUN WAYS TO BRING ON THE LAUGHTER

1. Surprise one another in fun, silly, or exciting ways! Tell him or her you'll be home a bit late, and then show up on time with flowers or a yummy dinner in hand.
2. Give your spouse a card with movie tickets in it, when they thought you had scheduled them a dental cleaning. If your spouse doesn't like the movies, there are many ways you can create a fun and thoughtful surprise to break up the routine and get a laugh together about the great joke.
3. Play some board or video games, but crank up the volume by betting something silly at home (such as, "Loser has to massage winner's feet!") or something sensual (such as, "Loser gives the other a massage anywhere they ask!").
4. Play an old familiar card game, but with speed rounds.
5. Send your spouse a silly note from a secret admirer that is obviously in your handwriting or from your email address!
6. Watch a favorite comedian together, and enjoy a snack while you watch.
7. Watch a funny movie you both like, or one from the past that you both like if you cannot find one from nowadays. If he or she won't watch with you, watch one yourself so you can feel less encumbered. Bring your good mood to your spouse when the energy is up and share the love!
8. Make a fun food for your time together. Being famished, parched, or completely staying away from occasional treats can contribute to grouchy attitudes.
9. If your mate is willing, exercise or walk together, which boosts positive brain function, and tell him or her about something funny that happened to you while you exercise.
10. Give each other blindfolded food taste tests to see if you can tell the difference between various sodas or chocolates of different brands, or discern between your pizza crust versus store bought crust, or anything else silly that can lighten up the everyday weeknight dinners.
11. Do a theme night for a game and dress up like characters from your own closet in five minutes or less, or make some sort of a contest out of it.

12. Tell each other a silly story using the same eight words, again and again, in various ways. Choose your words wisely!
13. Create a secret handshake or war whoop you can use when one of you has a victory.
14. Answer the phone using a funny voice when you call one another during the workday.
15. Make a plan to say NOTHING negative over the course of your RELATE time together, even if the comments are about others. Save that for the other one hundred and five hours of the week. On second thought, try not to say negative things at all.
16. Buy a joke or riddle book and read some of it together at mealtimes or before bed for a laugh.
17. Spend time with other couples that bring out the best in you and your spouse, but make sure some of your time is only for the two of you.
18. _____
19. _____
20. _____

ALL IN FUN OR CRYPTIC SARCASM?

After writing your list, it is important to remember that some jokes are masked as humor but are just plain mean. That there is a difference at all in types of humor may be eye opening to many couples since we don't usually stop to examine humor and its various aspects. However, there is humor that is either truly self or spouse deprecating, and that kind of humor should be cautiously avoided.

This is because at the root of this kind of sarcasm is the fear of rejection people have about themselves, such as, "I'm too fat to be attractive," or "I don't have a voice in this relationship," or many other unhealthy beliefs that shouldn't be laughed about. These can come out in well-intentioned humor, but it won't edify and offer life to the relationship the way healthy humor does, since it has fear of rejection at its root. Examples of the above sarcastic humor would be someone laughing while saying,

- "If I didn't look like a fat clown in this shirt, I'd look good," (Self-statement of a woman who feels she is too heavy), or
- "Can I use your head as a flashlight?" (Statement toward a husband who has lost his hair) or,
- "Of course you can have the money. You're the boss!" (As in the case of a husband who feels he has no financial voice but tries to cover it with humor).

If you say or have a lot of these self-deprecating thoughts about your relationship, put a stop to it, ask your spouse to stop it, and make a commitment to life-giving humor, even when in jest. *If you cannot stop the self or spouse loathing talk, counseling is appropriate, so you can kick the stinking thinking to the curb!*

However, in a healthy relationship, some types of sarcasm can be fun if well timed and placed. Here is an example. "Is it just me or is our kid filling her diaper the minute we change it?" In this case, you may only get a grunt of humor from your spouse versus a shared belly laugh, but it's still fun to joke around when it's not aimed at anyone who would mind, assuming your diapered baby is not a literary genius.

Ugly sarcasm may creep into the relationship from time to time, and you may not notice it as a big deal, but frankly, it doesn't add points to the score. In fact, it only increases fears and doubts about whether you or your mate are worthy of being loved. There are PLENTY of better ways for great fun in the relationship, as you can see in this book.

LAUGHTER AND CONFLICT TOGETHER

Laughter can even be brought right into or very soon after a conflict. Don't see how this can be possible? Think for a moment about an interaction you've had with one of your children, or child-aged relatives, in helping them to recover from a bad mood. If you don't know any kids, think of the ways some caring and fun-loving adult pulled you out of an angry mood when you were a child. We learn from the children in our lives that they can be awakened out of a frustrated mood fairly easily most of the time, excepting if they are exhausted. This can be done through tickle fests, telling a story for a distraction, burying them in hugs and kisses, or saying to one who is pouting, "I see that smile coming out!"

Just as you would work extra hard with a child to get them out of their bad mood, knowing how to push your spouse's theoretical "fun button" is just as important. If they are tired or cranky, don't try for a tickle fest (unless you really think it would work). Since I don't know your mate the way you do, it's up to you to take the time to learn your spouse's "fun button" to be able do it successfully, and you'll definitely want to have several tricks up your sleeve. Of course, by trying to be humorous, you don't want someone thinking you are not taking him or her seriously, but at the same time, you want him or her to know you care. Thus, be sure to respect their space if your spouse's fun button can only be approached after a good night's rest or a few hours. Be vulnerable and allow them to see your efforts in it, so they can help you in this discovery. Most likely they will be touched by the ways that you care for them even when you notice their unpleasant mood.

PLAN IT, DON'T CAN IT!

Although canned humor is totally lame, the message should now be clear that it is still important to plan fun into your marriage. Out of the one hundred and fifteen waking hours in week, you are dedicating roughly ten of them to be spent on having fun in your relationship.

This RELATE time comprises less than ten percent of your waking hours, and you care about this relationship more than any other. Plan some time to spend just relaxing and enjoying one another, and don't forget to insert laughter into other parts of the week also.

On the next page, list about five different times you will insert some silly fun into your week. Don't be legalistic about the time spent, but don't shortchange yourselves either. If you are hard workers, you definitely deserve some down time that's simply relaxing when you can let down and laugh a little or a lot!

How will we make life fun this week?

1. _____
2. _____
3. _____
4. _____
5. _____

QUICK REVIEW: PLAN FOR LAUGHTER

1. Complete your lists, starting with the funniest memories of your relationship. Share them together.
2. Commit to doing several fun or silly things each week in your marriage or relationship.
3. Avoid nasty or self-destructive sarcasm. Say only what is good for edification of others, especially your spouse! (See Ephesians 4:29 for this great biblical reminder).
4. Learn how to find your spouse's "fun button" to use as conflict is winding down or soon afterwards.
5. Plan specifically which fun things you will try in your relationship this week.

Hopefully you've had some romantic or otherwise loving sparks ignited by the playful exercises in the past few chapters. Now we will visit some of the hardest parts of your relationship, in hopes that you will bring along the tools you've learned so far to make your life more pleasant in the meantime.

CHAPTER 4

Accept Your Differences

Although building up your life together can be terrific fun, it also includes accepting the plain fact that all individuals, married or not, are different from one another. No two people are exactly the same, and some spouses are even inclined to be total opposites, which as you well know, often attract! After months or years of differences, sometimes our spouse's personality can wear on us as those differences appear less cute and more frustrating. If this has happened in your relationship, it's important to remember that you chose this person, in part, *because* they were different from you. In fact, they probably complemented your own character, which is great because your strengths in each area cause you to grow stronger together. Unfortunately, not all couples realize this until it is too late.

GIVING UP THE FIGHT

George and Tina were married for nineteen years. George married Tina for her beauty but also in large part because she was so bubbly and friendly with everyone she knew. He felt good that she had chosen him over the other men who had tried to win her, and he felt happy to have such a fun-loving, sparkling bride. Tina likewise felt happy to have picked George because he had a good head on his shoulders, and as a mature and studious young man, didn't spend time with just anyone. She felt honored when this handsome, quiet, smart and kind man chose her. For several years, these qualities continued to captivate George and Tina, along with many other great features they each brought to the table. However, after nineteen years, three kids, and a tight budget, Tina no longer thought George's strict, quiet nature was very cute, and George sure didn't think Tina's gabbing at all hours on the phone or begging him for conversation 24/7 was much fun either. They got a divorce, since they figured they were "wrong for each other," without realizing that their differences made for a great combo. They each re-married, only to find that a similar set of issues followed them into the next relationship as well.

How did this couple lose sight of the ways they complemented one another? They forgot, as most of us do at some time or other, that the differences between them and their mate created something very special; a unique dynamic, like two sides of a coin. Their children were also learning about how to balance hard work and fun through their parents' complementary personalities, which is a valuable lesson.

In both couples with and without children, the relationship dynamic influences the world in similarly significant and positive ways aside from family influence. For instance, one spouse may be organized and help a talented but less technologically-minded spouse to post their job resume all over online. A creative spouse may help a more linear thinker think of a new business to start. Differences offer the opportunity to fill in the gaps for each other also so each person has more to offer. Tina and George forgot to allow their differences to make them a much better team. This chapter will show you how to use your differences positively in your relationship, so you don't spend any more time on the negative and untrue idea that you're just "too different."

List ways you and your mate differ in terms of personality here and if your significant other is completing this exercise, ask him or her to complete this exercise after your list.

How do I see us differ?

1. _____
2. _____
3. _____
4. _____
5. _____

How does my spouse see us differ?

1. _____
2. _____
3. _____
4. _____
5. _____

Now that you've thought up plenty of differences, take a moment to find something positive that could come from each of your differences, even if it's a stretch. Write your answers on the following list. If you go back to Chapter One, you may interestingly notice that some of the things you wrote down about your differences here are represented on the list of what initially attracted you to your spouse in personality. In other words, your own and others' greatest weaknesses are also usually a flipside strength.

LOVE NOTE: *Take a moment to stir love by noting some of the positive aspects of your relationship differences. For example: Tina – outgoing – people respond well to her in public. George: Steady – People can depend on him to get a task done on time.*

What are some good ways we are different?

1. _____
2. _____
3. _____
4. _____
5. _____

Now use the space provided on the next page to write down five ways you can use your differences as a couple to bless one another, your family, or the world at large. (*Ex: George can make a steady wage for us so we have enough money to live if we budget well. Ex: Tina can plan fun social gatherings and thereby improve our quality of life.*)

How can we use our differences to bless one another?

1. _____
2. _____
3. _____
4. _____
5. _____

After doing this exercise, I hope you will see that your differences don't have to break you, but can be used to benefit you and the rest of the world also. However, some of your differences may actually be problem behaviors, and when this is the case, such as in the case of alcohol abuse or being an excessive spender, you need a more critical look at a solution, which will require sacrifice, willpower and a commitment. Make sure you use the healthy conflict management tools in Chapter Two to work together to come up with solutions for those things that are hurting your relationship and holding you both back tremendously.

You are not alone if you found several differences that still didn't sound all that great even after you did the above exercise. You wouldn't be human if everything were perfect after making the list, although it would be convenient. Even so, positive thinking *can* change you for good if you remember that your significant other, though different from you, adds a value to you, to your family, and to the world in a very different way than you do. As you come to terms with this truth, you can more freely use the list you created on the last page to inspire you as a couple to use your differences as a team. Whatever differences you have on the list that are not "Run and get counseling now" kind of difference, such as "He wants to be with someone else," or "She abuses the children," should be recognized as common to many couples.

LOVE NOTE: *People operate differently in the world, and no couple will love everything about one another. What you do with this common information is your choice. Choosing to love someone different from you can provide a wonderful opportunity for mutual growth.*

DEALING WITH MULTIPLE PROBLEMS AT ONCE

When your differences cause multiple conflicts, it can feel very overwhelming. Before you panic over the amount of problems you face, assess whether you are actually devoting ten or more hours a week to RELATE time. If you are, revisit the main points of each of the previous chapters so you can recharge, energize, and add laughter to your relationship to try to balance out the equation. If you are spending plenty of RELATE time together this week, and you have re-read the chapters but nothing seems to be working, call your best marriage support mentor, coach, pastor, or therapist. There is plenty of help available for the asking, and spending time and money on your most important relationship is worth it.

After you've done all you can and you still find differences that are difficult, it's often time to remember that loving a difficult spouse is an act of the will! Couples who spend their whole lives together rarely wish they'd divorced and left the other person. Instead, their character grows, and with dedication and effort, their marriage grows with it. Many who have stayed the course are thankful to have someone familiar who has stayed with them during their difficult moments, even if they didn't dazzle them with their everyday actions.

UNSOLVABLE PROBLEMS

It is also important to remember that after you've already tried everything else to convince your spouse of your point (i.e. "I just don't think fishing is as important as you do," or "I wish your mother wasn't so negative"), it is probably time to let that issue go for good. If your spouse isn't doing anything that goes against your top morals and values, try to remember that these kinds of "unsolvable problems" plague almost all couples. *Many couples find it comforting to remember that no two people agree on everything.* Sometimes you just have to learn to agree to disagree. If you can also laugh over your differences at times, you are really doing a terrific job of remembering that life goes by too fast to get hung up on the small stuff, and that humor can be the best of medicine.

QUICK REVIEW: YOUR PLAN OF ACCEPTANCE

1. Complete the lists in this chapter, which focus on how you and your significant other differ from one another and how those differences may be used for good.
2. Remember that your spouse's differences from you often complement you in important ways to strengthen you both.
3. Remember that no two people agree on everything. Ask God to meet your deepest needs and don't forget your self-care.
4. Remember to seek outside help for addictions or abuse.
5. Use the tools from Chapter Two for solving conflict when you come to differences that create difficulties.
6. Try to give up on solving the "unsolvable" relationship problems where there is no clear-cut right or wrong, and neither spouse is willing to bend. In cases where it does not compete with your morals, and an answer is needed, choose to compromise, take turns, or give in if it isn't an issue that would naturally hurt someone deeply. Pray that God would solve any "unsolvable" issues that need to be solved, for with God all things are possible (Matthew 19:26)!
7. Don't give up on spending time RELATE time together. Accepting our difference becomes well worth it when there is plenty of enjoyment as well.

In the next chapter, you will learn how to cope with trials as they come your way in the future. Loss, though difficult, can draw a couple much closer together in the long run if they don't give up.

CHAPTER 5

TRANSFORM THROUGH TRIALS

In *all* relationships if they last long enough, couples walk through many trials and difficult seasons of life together. Since trials come our way with or without marriage, we must remember that when the going gets tough, it is a privilege to journey together through life with one another. If we are married, it is our marital duty to faithfully toil with one another even when the "other" is not their typical self since they are sick, depressed, or in grief. If and when this happens to you, you *will* be asked to carry more than your share of the load financially, emotionally, physically, or in all of these ways. Although these times may be some of the most trying seasons in the course of life, being a great teammate in times of grief is essential for the long-term success of a healthy relationship and builds a godly, loving character in you as you learn to trust God more than ever.

In fact, if you throw in the towel in a time of crisis, you put your relationship in dire straits, as your marriage needs not just faithfulness, but *extra* efforts in times like this. The great news is, if you persevere during the tough seasons, you will transform through trials, and become a *much* stronger team in the end. You will come out stronger as individuals as well. Toiling through trials together is a win-win situation, and in this chapter, you will find additional support for the especially burdensome seasons of life. First, here are a few examples of major trials that occur in relationships at some time or another.

A FEW EXAMPLES OF MAJOR TRIALS:

- When a parent who is close to one or both mates dies.
- When a job is lost and/or finances are in shambles.

- When one spouse becomes ill, especially in the case of long-term disability, cancer, or another major illness.
- When a child is lost, has special needs, is very sick, or dies.
- When a couple is being sued.
- When a couple is going through bankruptcy.
- When a couple has experienced infidelity.
- When a spouse has had a traumatic experience.

As you read through the list, you may shudder at the thought of one of these disasters befalling you, or you may have a reminiscence of one of them that has previously happened to you, or that you are dealing with now. If so, don't skip over the reading just because it makes you uncomfortable. Everyone who has reached adulthood has had some grief experiences already, and you need tools to get through the hard times. In other words, if your relationship has already been touched by grief, you really need to pay attention here.

Take a moment to write out some times in your life when you have experienced grief. List up to five grief experiences, but try not to let the same problems hindering your relationship you listed in Chapter Two overlap too much, since you already made note of those issues. Instead, try to think about things that may more closely resemble grief (loss) versus annoyance or frustration. Following your list, there is a second list for a significant other who would like to do this exercise also.

LOVE NOTE: *Remember, you may recognize something as grievous, while your spouse does not (and vice versa), so don't tease him or her for writing down something you found to be trivial.*

When have I experienced grief in my life?

1. _____
2. _____
3. _____
4. _____
5. _____

When has my significant other experienced grief?

1. _____
2. _____
3. _____
4. _____
5. _____

After you have written down what the grief experiences have been, write some healthy ways you coped with each one below. How did you get through the tough times? Did your mate help you at all? If you are both working on this exercise, talk openly about what you needed during this time, what you got, who you got it from, and how you hope your significant other can be there for you in the future.

LOVE NOTE: *Do not shame a person who was, in your mind, not there for you during a grief experience. Your grief definitely altered not just you but also them for a time too, and therefore, your whole dynamic changed. Your mate was also adjusting to that change in your relationship, as well as to the grief situation. Instead, use the past behaviors and needs to inform your future together.*

Were there any unhealthy ways you dealt with the grief? If so, write those down also, and try to plan for better self-care next time. Be honest with your spouse about signals he or she can be aware of that may indicate you need help, like avoiding friendships or binge eating or drinking. See the examples here for help.

What are some healthy ways I have coped with grief?

1. _____
2. _____
3. _____
4. _____
5. _____

What are some unhealthy ways I have coped with grief?

1. _____
2. _____
3. _____
4. _____
5. _____

FACING A TRIAL TRIUMPHANTLY

Steve and Rose were a relatively happy couple for the first twelve years of marriage. Things changed dramatically when Steve had a back injury and consequentially lost his job. Though they had a bit of savings, there wasn't much money for fun, and Rose, a stay at home mother, had never worked outside of the home before. She wasn't exactly thrilled at the sudden prospect either, considering she was fulfilling an important job at home. The couple began to fight all the time, since Steve's intense pain was difficult to bear, Rose resented the transitions, and they had an enormous amount of financial stress.

In a few weeks, despite her discomfort, and at Steve's insistence, Rose agreed to go to work outside of the home. When Steve had reasonably recovered but was still laid off from work, he began to feel depressed. Rose consulted her pastor who encouraged her to make a doctor's appointment for Steve so he could be assessed for depression. This appointment helped Steve recognize his depression and he got medical and counseling treatment.

At their pastor's encouragement, Steve and Rose made a long-term family plan, which involved Rose continuing to work until Steve could get a job that paid the bills again. Steve continued to take his antidepressant medication faithfully, and did what he could do to help the kids with their homework and chores.

Steve and Rose also found creative ways to enjoy one another during their free time and Rose got some extra self care while she was out. Once a week, she went out to eat or to the movies with friends, so she would not feel like a round-the-clock caregiver while Steve recuperated and needed so much extra help. She also took daily power walks where she prayed and got some light exercise in.

By the time Steve had sufficiently recuperated, this couple had learned some valuable lessons about teamwork, and about not giving up even when the trials are intense. They also realized with pride that they could trust one another to transform through trials.

Here are a list of ways you and your spouse can sustain marital health and even grow closer as a couple in your times of grief. Included are things you can do individually and as a couple since, as mentioned earlier, there are many instances of grief where a spouse may not be much of a comfort because they are dealing with their own stress around the grief situation as well.

HEALTHY STRATEGIES FOR COPING WITH TRIALS

Circle *the options you would be willing to try if your significant other was going through a grief situation, and place a* **star** *next to the items you will try when you are experiencing grief also. Either way, for your relationship to thrive even during trials, commit to doing at least one of these items per day, depending on who has dealt with the loss. Add any ideas you've thought of at the end.*

1. Keep a journal, or read through letters from a lost loved one.
2. If the loss was largely your spouse's, bring it up from time to time, especially in the first year after the loss, and check in to see if they need some extra loving during this time or special anniversaries!
3. Be a good listener.
4. Grief can take a good six months or longer (for a death, grief is usually starting to improve after six months, but the first year or two can be very difficult), so for those first six months, which are often the most difficult, try to make sure you are getting good self-care.
5. Eat foods that will help you to thrive every two or three hours, even if you have to set alarm to remind yourself, or create a

meal planning schedule. You need this now more than ever since you will be tempted to eat junk or to avoid eating altogether. Indulge in a yummy treat sometimes, but not multiple times a day, which will be self-sabotaging in many ways.

6. Make sure to remember to support yourself and/or your spouse on anniversaries of the loss, such as the birthday of the person who died, as well as the date of death, as well as other special holidays where the person who is gone or changed will be grieved more fiercely.
7. Make a video, slideshow, or scrapbook for yourself or your spouse and allow the memories or positive moments to comfort and strengthen you.
8. Cry as needed, or hug the one who is crying.
9. Seek a counselor, a grief group, or a pastor who cares. This step is vital when the grief is just too overwhelming to you.
10. Spend time with a friend who cares about you and isn't afraid of your pain. If you're able, try to be there for them in their stories of pain also, as that can help distract you and help you to see others who are also dealing with loss.
11. Ask your church or neighborhood for support with meals and/or childcare.
12. As your friends and family for extended prayer support. In Matthew 18:19-20, Jesus reminds us that where two or more of His children are praying together, God is pleased beyond measure and present with us, answering those prayers!
13. Talk with someone ahead of you with a similar loss, such as a co-worker who lost his or her job, a parent who lost a child, another parent with a special-needs child who can offer hope, or a person who has lost a parent, spouse or sibling. Make sure to avoid toxic or thoroughly negative people as you look for support.
14. Ask for external family support, such as help with children, or even ask for some space if your extended family simply isn't helpful.
15. Take a step back from an overwhelming extracurricular leadership position if it is too much for you. Do not isolate yourself, as that will only make it worse. Just take some time away from extracurricular responsibilities, not the fellowship.

16. Have silly and fun times with children as much as you can, as kids can be such a wonderful distraction.
17. Ask a friend or family member to babysit for you weekly, so if you have children, you can have some space as well.
18. Read the Bible, especially the Psalms. This can be helpful especially since there are many laments from those saints who, while they walked this earth, dealt with trials of every kind. You will be reminded that God is compassionate towards those enduring trials, and still has a great plan for your life.
19. Exercise. This can help you with your sad mood, even if you are just going through the motions at the beginning.
20. Remember ways in which some trials may help you or others in the long run. You make new friends, find out who really loves you, and meet people you would not have otherwise met. A wonderful analogy of a loss is that of a large tree being cut off at the bottom of the trunk, leaving only a bare stump. The stump is ugly, causes people to trip, and takes up a lot of space. However, instead of allowing it to be a continual stumbling block, one can plant flowers and a pretty garden around that stump. Similarly, in grief, the pain will always be there, but the life you choose for yourself can still surround it and make it a beautiful life again, though the loss has changed the landscape.
21. Make a daily to-do list to keep yourself going, including reminders to love your spouse through the trials you face together. You may even need to write simple things on the list such as taking out the trash, eating, being affectionate towards your spouse, or showering since during a trial, everything except the pain can become cloudy.
22. Keep your life moving forward even while you mourn the past. Set goals for your work life each day also, however small.
23. If the loss was job related, and you need to find work quickly, continue to set small goals for each day, such as getting ready for cold calls, eating well, finding jobs online, and making phone calls, even though you feel upset. Ask your significant other for help in your job search, and while you are waiting for calls, use the time to learn a new skill in your trade to make you more marketable, especially if you think it's time for a new job in a field that interests you and is within your realistic capacity for work.

24. Commit to leaving a lasting legacy spiritually, emotionally, and financially to those you love during your precious years on Earth!
25. _____
26. _____
27. _____
28. _____

Refer back to this grief plan on your own or with your spouse, and if the trial is already at hand, keep this section ready and available for times when you need reminders of the simple things. In any case, be encouraged. Though there is weariness at times in life, joy and hope will return after a season if you just keep moving forward!

QUICK REVIEW: TRANSFORMATION PLAN

1. Complete the lists in this chapter to help you recognize trials you have gotten through. Name the coping strategies that helped you along.
2. Be honest about the ways you were unhealthy in your previous coping styles, and plan on your own or discuss with your spouse ways you plan to beat anything that comes your way again. Ask your spouse to be aware of certain desires for help in a time of need.
3. Place a star next to several healthy coping strategies from the list provided for you that you will do when you have a trial, to maintain self and family care as best as possible. This includes letting others carry as much as possible for you. Place a circle next to the ways you will love your mate when they experience trials. Make sure you do at least one of these items per day, depending on who is struggling the most. If you are both struggling, do something for each of you every day.
4. Allow the strengths to transform you into a tougher, more resilient team who can get through anything together!
5. Remember that as Christians who have the promise of eternal life, our grief can heal with hope! (1st Thessalonians 4:13).

Now that you have decided you will not allow the inevitable seasons of grief and loss to weaken your relationship, you are ready to move on to one final topic; learning how to engage your spouse or mate. In other words, you'll learn to turn boring everyday dialogue into captivating conversation!

CHAPTER 6

ENGAGE ONE ANOTHER

When you're working on making your marriage or relationship more satisfying, one final component that you absolutely must not forget is to be engaging! Being engaging means to be charming, winning, attractive and pleasing. Anyone can possess these qualities, no matter what raw physical qualities they bring to the table.

LOVE NOTE: *Be encouraged. Even if you think you are past your "glory years," captivating couples comes in all shapes, sizes, and ages.*

Although the other qualities we've discussed in this RELATE program are important, having an engaging dynamic can take a relationship from good to great! This is because engaging couples are the doers of the world. They are the ones who are thriving, as opposed to the ones who are merely surviving.

An example of couples or individuals who are merely surviving are the many who stay at home or go to work but have no real zest for their chores, jobs or any meaningful connections. They come home to watch TV for the night without contributing to interesting conversations. They don't make small talk with others, they don't play with kids they happen to know (or have!), and they don't show excitement or passion about things. Everyone fall into ruts sometimes, but if you or your spouse makes survival-only living a habit, you are missing out on great experiences will allow you both to thrive!

LOVE NOTE: *Don't label someone who is exhausted, in grief, sick or clinically depressed as someone who is not engaging. These individuals are usually in need of rest, time to grieve, medication* *and/or counseling before they will improve. Use discernment to know whether someone is ready or willing to make change. If so, ask, don't push. Even if you alone change for the better, you're off to a great start to kick off potential change in someone else, or at least to enjoying life more yourself!*

Follow the few steps listed here to assess and make sure you are every bit as engaging in your relationship as you'd like your significant other to be.

- First of all, to be engaging, you have to be interested in the world. If you have no interests or passions, then it's very difficult to be engaging.
- Ask yourself what interests you in life and in the world. Whether it's politics or gourmet cooking, helping needy children, playing tennis, or crocheting, is there anything you do or enjoy thinking about that brings you some level of interest and excitement? If so, list these things here:

What am I passionate about?

1. _____
2. _____
3. _____
4. _____
5. _____

As always, if your mate is completing the exercise with you, give them the opportunity to write in the things they feel passionate about as well, by sharing their interests in the space provided here.

What is my mate passionate about?

1. _____
2. _____
3. _____
4. _____
5. _____

Now that you have ideally both shared things you are passionate about, you have several topics to help you in your quest to become engaging. Though it would be unrealistic to think about or talk about these things all of the time, knowing what each of you are passionate about lends itself to readily interesting conversation topics. Here, create one final list which includes things you are both passionate about. If you don't have any, that's okay, but if so, these make for more naturally engaging conversation starters.

What are some things we are both passionate about?

1. _____
2. _____
3. _____
4. _____
5. _____

HOW TO LEAD AN ENGAGING CONVERSATION

With your topics in mind, having an engaging conversation is pretty easy. Use your mate's topics frequently to create a more engaging discussion dynamic. If you notice, for example, that your spouse wrote that he or she is passionate about baseball (or you already know this about him or her), do some brief Internet research for five or ten minutes, and find out something new about the sport. Bring it up in conversation. Be engaging with it, not simply conversational.

Someone who is engaging would not say, "Hey! You haven't talked to me since we got home. Want to talk about baseball?" It just doesn't sound natural, and a phony or whiny way of engaging will come across as just that. Instead, if baseball is the chosen topic, the engaging spouse might say, "I noticed that the [name of baseball team] is in 1st place right now. I can't believe that comeback! From what I've heard you say, they didn't stand a chance last year!" If the listening spouse likes baseball and is making even a small effort, he or she will positively respond to this thoughtful, energetic, and engaging conversation starter.

RELATE: A Guide to Marriage & Relationship Repair

LOVE NOTE: *When your spouse responds to you, listen up. This means showing care toward their interests and consideration toward their opinions. It also involves attempting to connect with them as a person while you cover the topic, since nonverbal communication may be even more powerful than the words being said. Remember: Be conversational, not controversial, so you don't end up arguing.*

One specific example of an engaging person is a man who is the spouse of a children's Sunday School teacher. Since he knows that his spouse loves teaching children, he frequently ask a question about it while they are driving home from the church, such as, "What kind of fun games did you play with your kids in class today?" After listening well and complimenting his spouse for any good leadership traits he noticed, he may add a story from his own school days, or at other times, ask her about her days as a student in the classroom. His wife reminisces about games from the old days to bring into her classroom, and moreover really finds his questions engaging, as would any person in a conversation so thoughtfully woven in this direction. This spouse consistently shows care towards his wife's interests in other areas of life also. She is a happier wife, a better teacher from this engaging, encouraging conversationalist, and her students are undoubtedly blessed by her creative and confident attitude as well.

THE RULES OF ENGAGEMENT

Though there are countless other examples of being engaging, innovative and creative in conversations, a very basic rule of thumb for being engaging is to do the following at least once per day. Ask your mate to do the same for you.

1. Choose a topic your mate enjoys.
2. Ask open-ended questions about it.
3. Listen well.
4. Use words and non-verbal cues to show genuine interest.

LOVE NOTE: *If your mate is not interested in being an engaging spouse toward you, and is unwilling or forgetful about trying this exercise on you, try to bring up one of your own interests* *in an engaging way each day, since they won't be talked about unless you try, and it still may bring up a great discussion.*

One litmus test of noticing whether you are truly engaging someone is to examine whether they keep checking their watch, looking at the TV, or checking their phone. If they keep doing these things, either go back to the drawing board of trying a new topic, find a new way of broaching the same topic, or if you've exhausted all options, try again later. If your mate is a mature adult, you don't need to whine that they should pay attention to you. Instead, be interesting enough to engage them. Whatever positive thing you do to get your mate's attention, don't stop trying, because encouraging your spouse to be passionate about both of your gifts and interests is never a waste. He or she, like you, has things to share with this world, and everyone, *especially* your teammate in life, needs someone who believes in them.

THE LOOK OF ENGAGEMENT

Another aspect of being engaging involves putting your best foot forward in relationships. In the physical sense this simply means being intentional about taking good care of yourself, so you feel good, so you have more health and energy, and so you can be more confident toward your spouse and others. You don't have to get manicures constantly, or spend time in the tanning booth (you probably shouldn't do the latter, anyway!), but you should shower daily, make sure your clothes are free from food stains and wrinkles, and that your hair is combed and styled each day. You should try to eat foods that allow you to thrive on a regular basis, even if you enjoy splurging on occasion. These practices will not guarantee your significant others' enticement, but if you have a healthy attitude about the way you look, your significant other *will* notice it. Even though they will certainly see your flaws (they do live with you after all!) those flaws will become less prominent in their view, since you do the best with what you've got!

INSPIRE & INFLUENCE OTHERS

Now that you've created a list of what engages not only your spouse, but yourself also, make sure that you also talk about your own interests *in an engaging way*. Don't keep the passion you have for conversations with only your friends, siblings or parents, and save the "coupon conversation" for your spouse. An example of coupon conversation is simply talking about the everyday stuff of life, like "Milk's on sale this week, you notice?" or "Is it garbage day already again?" Some of this type of conversation is essential, so you maintain a responsible team balance. If, however, it is to the exclusion of interesting topics, you are missing the fact that you and your spouse were made to bring companionship and joy to one another more than any friend or sibling can do for either of you!

Instead, let your significant other know when you've got something interesting going on, by pulling them in naturally. When you have enthusiasm for a topic of your own, wait for the right moment and tell them about the interesting conversation you had, something new you learned, or the idea or a dream you have that could make money one day, with his or her input helping you along. Everyone feels good about being consulted, and if you manage to hook your mate into the conversation, dreaming together can be great fun.

Another way of going about the rules of engagement, especially with a less passionate spouse, is to focus in on talking mostly about the dreams or passions you share, consulting from your list in this chapter as needed. For example, if you are both trying to lose weight or get into shape, you could say, "I'm so glad I heard about a new workout routine at the gym. It really shocked me when I saw a gal I know who looks fantastic after doing it for only one month." If you've gotten your spouse's attention, your relationship can thrive more authentically. Remember the phrase, "Go big or go home." Keep it in mind for yourselves as you strive to achieve your dreams of connecting well, one engaging conversation at a time.

BE A DOER, NOT A VIEWER

Now that you are well on your way to functioning as a healthier individual and couple, it's time to take the first steps toward those plans and dreams (things you are passionate about) that you wrote down in this chapter. Consult the relationship goals you wrote about back in Chapter One.

For example, if you are a couple who have a goal for more recreational time together, and you also like baseball, could you join a church team together? Could you write about it, be an umpire for Little League, play or invite your family to your games? Could your family business sponsor the church team or could you coach a team? Not everything you are passionate about has to be done, or done together for that matter, but if you want to be an engaging, goal-reaching individual and couple, you need to be doers in the world, not just viewers. You are alive for many good reasons, to love God and others, to work hard, and to enjoy using your gifts and talents, whatever they may be!

If your mate is reticent to get involved with the first few things you suggest, don't give up. *The importance of at least some recreation together cannot be underestimated.* However, if they truly won't do anything that is mutually enjoyable, don't wait for them to join you in engaging in bird watching, tennis lessons, or gourmet cooking classes. Instead, save up the money to do it (or find something that interests you that is also free), offer it to your spouse as an open option, and then go and do it yourself whether he or she goes or not.

Don't let age hold you back either. You are never too old to make life interesting, no matter what your physical limitations, budget or constraints. The choice is up to you! Be engaging to your significant other, but also to yourself! You are not an enslaved victim. You are a talented individual, and you are worth it. Your mate and the world at large will be blessed by your individual and mutual investments alike.

If you bring hard work and a good attitude into whatever project or task you've got in front of you, you'll be a better worker and naturally find family or friends who support you. If you also bring joy, a captivating attitude, and your engaging personality to those around you, you'll have people wanting you to work with or for them, friends who really want to spend time with you, couples who want a marriage like yours, and a spouse who truly admires you.

QUICK REVIEW: PLAN TO ENGAGE

1. Complete the lists in this chapter that help you and your spouse to identify any individual or shared passions.
2. Recognize that someone who is engaging toward others is caring, considerate, and strives for connection in conversation.
3. Remember that even if your significant other doesn't join you in becoming more engaging at the onset, your enthusiasm and positive attitude, as well as your charming and attractive manner for engaging them will likely lead to their own transformation.
4. When you are trying to pull others into your own engaging life interests, make sure you find a way to connect with them, so that your discussion also includes ways they may want to get involved, or ways they have inspired you. Pray together about finding a common goal or mission!
5. Don't be a victim if your mate isn't willing to join you in life's pursuits. Don't be codependent on someone else for fun, but instead find simple, healthy, and pleasing interests that will help you to personally find refreshment, and ultimately make your home and this world a better place.

In our closing chapter, we will look at the complete picture of what it means to be a team who really knows how to relate! Then you can keep moving forward on the journey toward a much more satisfying relationship!

CHAPTER 7

Ready, Set, Relate!

Congratulations! You've put several hours, days, or possibly even weeks into refreshing and repairing what is possibly the most important relationship you have on earth. During this time, you've learned how to do the following:

- R – Recharge your marriage and love life,
- E – Energize, keeping the life flowing into your relationship,
- L – Laugh and have fun in your marriage,
- A – Accept that you are different but complementary,
- T – Transform into a closer couple through trials, &
- E – Engage one another with captivating conversations!

SHHHH!...
USE DISCRETION TO PROTECT THE RELATIONSHIP

Now, since you are working on goals to create a healthy relationship, you are both rare and enviable. This is because most people unfortunately go with the currents of life, even when that means metaphorically sinking versus swimming in a marriage. These people often give out way too many details of their relationship hurts without giving a second thought to how that may be damaging to themselves, to their relationship, and to the listener.

If you want to heal, thrive and love for years and years, to avoid temptations, and to maximize your potential as a couple, you must carefully avoid common but disastrous pitfalls. Here are a few tips for keeping a healthy circle of protection around your relationship.

1. **Don't gossip about the relationship.** If you gossip about your relationship, some people, even family, can be very manipulative with it. Word can get back to your mate that you were bad-mouthing them. Also, this sharing may actually make you feel worse about your mate and your feelings and acts of love may decrease from repeating and naming his or her offences aloud (This of course excludes revealing abuse, in which case you should always report.). When you feel like gossiping just to "vent," instead use the time you would have wasted on it to love yourself (and if you can muster it up, your mate) in a tangible way instead.
2. **Keep the details of your intimate and sexual relationship private.** This means keeping bedroom topics in the bedroom, or within the private bounds of a marriage therapist, coach, or trusted and agreed upon mentor, especially if things are out of control or not going well.
3. **Listen to your instinct about friendships with the opposite sex.** If you think a friend or colleague flirts with or admires you a little too much, make sure you listen to your gut feelings about this situation and back off. This goes double if you find yourself returning the flirtation. If you don't generally feel this way about others, it's probably because there is something off about the relationship. Avoid hanging out, making small talk at work, emailing, or chatting on the phone with them, and confess your feelings about this person. If your significant other also has a friendship with this person, ask them to back off as well. It's far better to be with people who show the utmost respect for your relationship by not flirting with you. This does not mean trying to find friends who are unattractive or never speaking to an attractive person of the opposite sex. It does mean listening for cues to know when you have gone too far in your behaviors and/or fantasy life about this person,

getting accountability from a friend who respects your relationship, and making the commitment to back off. Your relationship does not have a fair chance at surviving, much less thriving, if in your heart, you are always comparing your partner with someone else.

4. **Use common sense.** Similarly, if you become close friends with someone you know your spouse or mate is attracted to, *and* this friend is also flirtatious, it's really difficult to expect your spouse not to feel tempted. Use common sense and wisdom in keeping and letting go of unhealthy relationships with other individuals who are attractive to your mate.

5. **Leave your biggest worries and fears with God.** Trust God's Word, the Bible, to guide you in situations where you need wisdom, and accept that if and when your spouse or mate hurts you, this is normal. No two human beings agree about everything, or "never fight," unless they never speak! If you strongly fear abandonment and live out of that fear versus trusting God for your care at the end of the day, you will not be able to allow your spouse to freely love you. Instead you will be trying to control and manipulate them. Let go of them enough so that he or she can choose to love you freely. In the meantime, pray for your relationship and do what you can to be an attractive spouse, inside and out. Take care of yourself in healthy ways, so the burden for your very survival is not continually on your spouse. In other words, don't forget the three components of self-care each day: physical, spiritual, and emotional refreshment.

STANDING THE TEST OF TIME

Now that you have finished learning to RELATE, you have a lifetime to put your training to the test! As you move through the journey united as a team, remember, no two individuals will ever relate perfectly with one another, so don't be surprised by the bumps in the road created by your conflicts. When you hit a roadblock, remember the wonderful teammate that has helped you through so many things in your life, and don't give on them, yourself, or your relationship! Refer back to the lessons you learned from this book from time to time, so you can learn from the lists you made for a healthy life together!

Remember, if you are married, marriage is more than just two individuals, but is comprised of two individuals who have become one, and together have created something completely different and more powerful than what they were before intertwining. You are here to shape the world jointly. Though sometimes you are apart, and sometimes you have different roles in the relationship, you are ultimately a better team together!

Author's Note:

If and when you face something that feels like it is beyond the scope of this book, look to the Bible and the ultimate Life Coach, God, to help you in your trials, for He alone can give you the strength and wisdom to move past the seemingly insurmountable issues in your life. Please also seek professional counsel if you are in an abusive relationship or are dealing with emotions that seem out of control.

If you have enjoyed this book and would like to continue enriching your marriage, consider going through my *RELEASE* book next, which gives a deeper understanding of marital struggle and many more tools for triumph. It is available on Amazon.com along with my other publications.

Please feel free to contact me at **christa@reflectionscc.com** if you have questions, comments, or would like prayer or help for your marriage or family.

Special thanks to Wes Hardin, my awesome hubby who edited this book for me (and much more, has been my best friend through it all!)

Printed in Great Britain
by Amazon